¡Hola Córdoba!
A Kid's Guide To Córdoba, Spain

Photography By John D. Weigand
Poetry By Penelope Dyan

Bellissima Publishing, LLC
Jamul, California
www.bellissimapublishing.com

copyright © 2012 by Penny D. Weigand & John D. Weigand

All rights reserved. No part of this book may be reproduced or transmitted in any form or by any means, electronic or mechanical, including photocopying, recording, or by any other means, or by any information or storage retrieval system, without permission from the publisher.

ISBN 978-1-61477-035-0
First Edition

> "Pigmies placed on the shoulders of giants see more than the giants themselves."
>
> Lucan (November 03, 0039-)
> Spanish Poet

¡ Hola Córdoba!
Bellissima Publishing, LLC

Introduction

Córdoba was an Iberian and Roman city in ancient times. In the Middle Ages it became the capital of an Islamic caliphate. The old town contains many architectural reminders of its past. Some say in the 10th century and at the beginning of the 11th century, that Córdoba was the most populous city in the world and the intellectual center of Europe. That said, it is most definitely a beautiful place to see with many things that will interest kids of all ages, even kids who happen to be adults!

Take a walk across the bridge and go into the old part of the city with award winning author, attorney and former teacher, Penelope Dyan, and look through the lens of photographer John D, Weigand to see some of the things you can see and do in this exciting city. Take some pictures of your own and make your own book, and collect postcards and souvenirs and make them a part of your story. And look for a free Penelope Dyan music video on YouTube that goes with this book, and a web show for children on www.stop4fun.org to enhance the learning experience. Use all of these things and put them in your tool chest of learning, and do not stop there. Learn everything you can and explore, whether in person or vicariously using all the tools at your disposal! Most of all, have fun! Because learning is fun!

¡Hola Córdoba!
Bellissima Publishing, LLC

¡Hola Córdoba!
A Kid's Guide To Córdoba, Spain

Photography By John D. Weigand
Poetry By Penelope Dyan

The old part of the city
lies straight ahead.*
It looks mysterious and intriguing,
and you are glad you got out of bed.
And even though you were tired
from traveling all night,
the beauty of THIS place
makes everything right!

*View of the Roman bridge (Torre de la Calahorra) and the city of Córdoba. The Roman Bridge over the Guadalquivir River was built in the early 1st century BC, during the period of Roman rule in Córdoba. This ancient bridge is approximately 250 meters long and has 16 arches.

As you walk over the ancient bridge,
you see this old mill house stand.
It ground the grains that grew,
in this old ancient land.

There is an old mill water wheel*
hidden deep within dried brush.
You want to stop and look.
Mom says, "There is no rush."

*The Guadalquivir river-bed is wide enough for small islands which today are only inhabited by birds. Long ago there used to be flour mills, of which some remains can still be seen to this day..

At the end of the bridge you find
another tall and ancient tower.*
It is now a beautiful museum.
Dad says, "Knowledge is its power."

* This is the Torre De La Calahorra, and it is now a museum. .

And then you finally reach,
the city's arched gate.*
You start to run.
Mom says, "Please wait!"

* An Arab gate stood here until 1571, when the mayor ordered the construction a new gate to commemorate King Felipe II's visit to Cordoba. The new gate was designed by Hernan Ruiz III, who had also worked with his father on the construction of the cathedral. The gate is called Puerta del Puente.

Along the Mesquita Mosque,
(now a Cathedral wall*)
you look as you walk.
Your mother says,
"Oh, if only walls could talk. . .
Oh, the history they could tell;
and they would know it VERY well."

* The Mezquita dates back to the 10th century when Córdoba reached its zenith under a new emir, Abd ar-Rahman III who was one of the great rulers of Islamic history. This place is also called Cathedral Street.

There is a man with a white
scarf on his head,
playing an instrument orange and red.
He sits upon a chair of green,
It's one of the most interesting
things you've heard or seen.

The bell tower* stands proud and tall.
You wonder if you've seen it all.
It's Sunday and the church bells ring,
from inside you hear the choir sing.

*The Torre de Alminar is 93 meters high and was built on the site of the original minaret. It is possible to climb the steps to the very top, if that is something you would like to do.

They sell Spanish porcelain
against a wall nearby.
Mom says it's so beautiful
that she wants to cry.
Instead dad buys her a beautiful pot,
even though he says it costs a lot!

You look down a long narrow street,*
and your little heart skips a beat.
You say, "I'm tired. I need to rest."
Mom says, "Keep walking,"
and (after all) mom does know best!
And so you keep moving ahead
with your two little feet,
and you keep right on walking
down that long narrow street!
You see a dog, and you see a cat.
You see this, and you see that.

*This is one of the many streets of the Cordoba Historic Centre.

Then you turn a corner and you see even more!
And you and mom go into a store.
You buy matching aprons
(after taking a look)
Mom says you'll wear them,
when you go home and cook.
You think the idea is really neat;
and Dad likes the idea,
because HE likes to EAT!

The lights come on
with the setting sun,
and you are kind of sad
the day's all done.
But tomorrow is a brand new day,
and tomorrow you'll be on your way;
you'll get on the train
and you'll clickety clack
down that track;
but you aren't worried.
Because someday. . . you'll be back.

"Teach thy tongue to say
'I do not know,'
and thou shalt progress."

Maimonides (March 30, 1135 - December 13, 1204)

www.ingramcontent.com/pod-product-compliance
Ingram Content Group UK Ltd.
Pitfield, Milton Keynes, MK11 3LW, UK
UKHW060133240426
12048UKWH00002B/19